D0893852

Humanitarians

Janice Parker

Weigl

CALGARY

www.weigl.com

Dedication

This series is dedicated to all Canadians who take pride in their communities and their citizenship; and to those who will continue to help build a strong Canada. The Canadians in this series have helped to build Canada by being outstanding in their fields, from literature to business, sports to the arts. Some have overcome great obstacles to make their dreams come true, and their dedication and achievement serve as an inspiration for young and old alike.

Published by Weigl Educational Publishers Limited
6325 – 10 Street SE
Calgary, Alberta, Canada
T2H 2Z9
Website: http://www.weigl.com
Copyright © 2000 WEIGL EDUCATIONAL PUBLISHERS LIMITED

Canadian Cataloguing in Publication Data

Parker, Janice.
    Great Canadian humanitarians

(Great Canadians)
Includes bibliographical references and index.
ISBN 1-896990-88-6

    1. Social reformers—Canada—Biography—Juvenile literature. 2. Philanthropists—Canada—Biography—Juvenile literature. I. Title. II. Series: Great Canadians (Calgary, Alta.)
HV107.P37 2000   j361.92'271   C00-910052-0

Printed in Canada
1 2 3 4 5 6 7 8 9 0   04 03 02 01 00

Editor
Rennay Craats
Design
Warren Clark
Cover Design
Terry Paulhus
Copy Editor
Heather Kissock
Layout
Lucinda Cage

Photograph Credits

Every reasonable effort has been made to trace ownership and to obtain permission to reprint copyright material. The publishers would be pleased to have any errors or omissions brought to their attention so that they may be corrected in subsequent printings.

Ed Broadbent: pages 7, 8; Rosemary Brown: pages 13, 14, 16; June Callwood: pages 18, 19, 20, 21, 22, 23; CP Picture Archive: pages 6, 10, 11, 17, 30, 44; Glenbow Archives: page 41; Kielburger Family: pages 32, 33, 34, 35; Max Bell Foundation: page 42; McGill University Archives: page 25; National Archives of Canada: pages 36, 40, 45; New Democratic Party of Canada: page 9; The Province: page 15; Provincial Archives of Alberta: pages 38, 39; Paul Ritchi: page 31; Terry Fox Foundation: page 43; UN/DPI: pages 24, 26, 27, 28, 29; Barbara Woodley: page 12.

CONTENTS

6
Ed Broadbent

12
Rosemary Brown

18
June Callwood

24
John Humphrey

30
Craig Kielburger

36
Emily Murphy

MORE GREAT CANADIANS

Max Bell 42

Thomas Berger 42

Gladys Cook 42

Jules Deschênes 43

Terry Fox 43

Rick Hansen 43

Wilson Head 44

Izaak Killam 44

Stephen Lewis 44

Robert McClure 45

Mary Two-Axe Earley 45

Georges Vanier 45

Glossary 46

Suggested Reading 47

Index 48

Humanitarians

Throughout history, Canada as a nation has had a reputation for being a peacekeeping country that supports humanitarian causes worldwide. Humanitarians are people who work to improve the lives of other people. Some humanitarians take on difficult tasks in order to help others. Craig Kielburger, for example, campaigns to stop child labour around the world.

Some Canadian humanitarians have devoted their lives to helping others by protecting basic **civil rights**. Many of the people in this book fought to protect the rights of various minority groups in Canada, such as women, visible minorities, or Aboriginal peoples. Others, such as John Humphrey, worked internationally to help protect the human rights of people around the world.

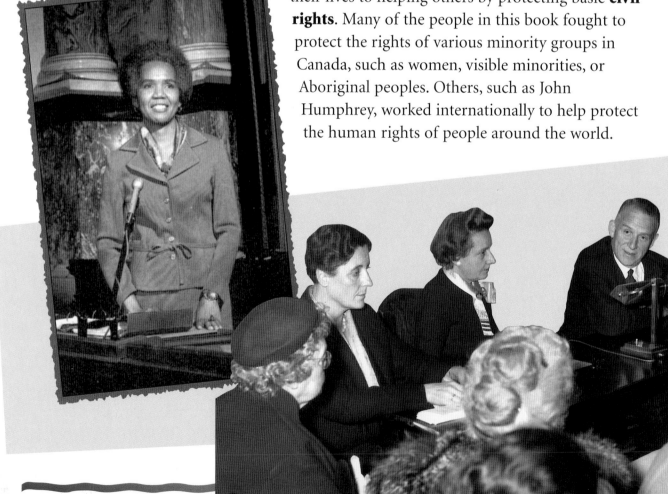

Humanitarians are also people who donate time and money to causes that help people. **Philanthropists** have funded programs that improve Canadians' quality of life.

Canadians have proven to the world that they care about humans and human rights. Citizens of all ages and all backgrounds have made a difference to people in Canada and the world. Some of these people are well respected internationally. Others are well known mainly in Canada. There are some people who you may not be familiar with and others you may have heard about before. Each of the people in this book has dedicated his or her life in some way to protecting and improving the lives of Canadians and others around the world. Their stories may inspire you to make a difference by helping others.

1936–

Ed Broadbent

> " Our social rights are taken as rights of citizenship today, but since the nineties, governments have attacked these rights. And, if they have not been verbally attacked, they are certainly being reduced or cut back. "

Key Events

1955 Graduates from high school and is class valedictorian

1961 Joins the New Democratic Party (NDP)

1966 Receives doctorate in political studies

1968 Elected as member of Parliament (M.P.) for Oshawa

1975 Is elected leader of the NDP

1990 Becomes founding president of the International Centre for Human Rights and Democratic Development (ICHRDD)

1993 Is named Officer of the Order of Canada

1995 Establishes truth and justice commission in Haiti

1996 Steps down as president of ICHRDD

1996 Takes on fellowship at Oxford University

1997 Becomes visiting professor at Simon Fraser University

Early Years

Ed Broadbent was born in Oshawa, Ontario. As a boy, he enjoyed playing baseball and hockey. He also did very well at school. Ed was a responsible boy as well. He was a boy scout and had a job as a paper delivery boy for several years.

Ed was always an excellent student. He was elected student council president when he was in the eleventh grade. He was valedictorian in his final year of high school. After graduation, Ed attended Trinity College at the University of Toronto. In college, Ed studied philosophy and developed an interest in political theory.

After receiving his degree, Ed taught high school for a year. He then returned to university to do graduate studies. In 1961, he moved to England, where he attended the London School of Economics. Ed returned to Toronto in 1966 and received his **doctorate** in political studies. He then became a professor at York University.

When Ed graduated from university in 1959, he was first in his class.

Backgrounder

London School of Economics

The London School of Economics (LSE) is a school in London, England. The LSE was founded in 1895, and it is known around the world for its excellence in teaching and research in social, political, and economic studies. Another Canadian who attended this school and then went on to great success is former prime minister Pierre Trudeau.

Developing Skills

While Ed was a university instructor, the New Democratic Party (NDP) asked him to run for office in the 1968 election. Ed agreed and began **campaigning** in his hometown. Ed was not a good public speaker and had little political experience. Despite this, his enthusiasm helped him win the election. Ed beat an experienced politician and won a seat in the federal Parliament by just fifteen votes.

Two years after Ed was elected, the leader of the NDP, Tommy Douglas, decided to step down from his position. Ed campaigned to become the new NDP leader. At the 1971 leadership convention, Ed failed at this attempt, losing to David Lewis by many votes.

In 1974, the NDP did poorly in the federal election and David Lewis lost his seat in Parliament. The NDP asked Ed to temporarily become leader of the party. Ed was no longer sure if he wanted to be the leader of the party. He felt that the position might take him away from his family too much.

Tommy Douglas (right) was the first NDP premier of Saskatchewan. He helped Ed (centre) in his election campaign.

Backgrounder

New Democratic Party

The NDP is a political party that believes in social democracy. The party began as the Co-operative Commonwealth Federation (CCF) in 1933. The CCF was popular during the Great Depression because of its social programs. In 1961, the CCF became the NDP. Although the NDP has never had much power nationally, it has helped influence the social programs in Canada by forming governments in several provinces. The NDP was once considered the "third party" in Canada, after the Progressive Conservatives and the Liberals.

In 1975, Ed decided to run for the party leadership. It was a close race against Rosemary Brown, but Ed won. Over the next few years, he made the NDP stronger. In order to improve his popularity with the public, his advisors suggested a few changes. Ed learned how to better speak in front of microphones and cameras, and he updated his wardrobe. In 1977, Ed was **unanimously** re-elected as leader of the NDP.

Ed and the NDP also became more popular with Canadians. In 1980, thirty-two NDP members were elected to Parliament, more than ever before. Ed also began to do some international work. As vice-president of an organization called Socialist International, Ed travelled to Guatamala and El Salvador to assess the civil wars in the areas.

In 1988, Ed and the NDP got forty-three seats in Parliament. In public opinion polls, more Canadians said they wanted Ed as prime minister than any other party leader.

Many people thought that Ed would have been prime minister if he was a member of the Conservative or Liberal Party.

66 Access to health care and pension systems that let people retire with dignity are worth defending. They should be for everyone in terms of what it means to be a citizen—not just a safety net for the people. 99

Accomplishments

In 1989, Ed decided to move away from politics. In his final speech in Parliament, Ed made a plea that the government end child poverty in Canada by the year 2000. This motion was passed unanimously in the House of Commons.

The following year, the Canadian government created the International Centre for Human Rights and Democratic Development (ICHRDD). Prime Minister Brian Mulroney appointed Ed as the first president of the organization. In his position at the ICHRDD, Ed was a supporter of human rights and democracy around the world. As president, Ed travelled around the world. He and the ICHRDD have been active in supporting democracy in Burma, Haiti, and many other developing countries. In 1993, he went to Burma to try to convince the government there to release Aung San Sui Kyi, the leader of the National League for Democracy.

Ed's concern over social problems in Canada and around the world spurs him to action. He speaks to governments and citizens about poverty, health care, and human rights.

Backgrounder

The International Centre for Human Rights and Democratic Development (ICHRDD)

In 1988, the Canadian government decided to create an independent international organization to support universal human rights and democracy worldwide. The ICHRDD focusses on furthering women's rights and the rights of indigenous peoples around the world. The organization awards the John Humphrey Freedom Award each year to an exceptional person who has worked to protect global human rights.

That same year, Ed was one of four international judges on the Tribunal of Violations of Women's Rights at the United Nations Conference on Human Rights in Vienna. The following year, Ed was on a panel of experts on the International Tribunal on Rights in Haiti. He also helped create and acted as an advisor to Haiti's National Truth and Justice Commission, which looked into human rights violations in that country. Ed was also active in calling for effective UN intervention in Rwanda and other human rights crises.

In 1993, Ed was named an Officer of the Order of Canada for his international activities in support of human rights. He left his position at the ICHRDD in 1996 for a one year **fellowship** at Oxford University in England. In the fall of 1997, Ed took on a two year position as chair of the Institute of Humanities at Simon Fraser University in Vancouver, British Columbia. In this position, he conducted research and taught democracy, rights, and citizenship.

Throughout his career, Ed has been vocal about the connection between international trade and human rights. He has said, "If we now use trade agreements to protect property rights, surely it is time we used them to protect the rights of people affected by that trade."

Ed is active in Campaign 2000, which is an effort to end child poverty in Canada.

> It is in the best interest, throughout this globe, to make human rights obligations a key component in all regional and global trade agreements.

QUICK NOTES

- Ed enjoys listening to classical music and watching movies.
- Ed played a mobster on one episode of the television series *Sirens*.
- Ed published a book of political essays called *The Liberal Rip-Off*.

1930–

Rosemary Brown

> 66 Canada is a country where people have come from all over the world. That's always been our history and I think it's a good history. That is our reality, that is our goal. 99

Key Events

1950 Moves to Canada to attend university in Montreal

1955 Graduates, moves to Vancouver, and marries Bill Brown

1972 Is elected to the British Columbia **legislature**

1975 Runs for the leadership of the federal New Democratic Party

1986 Retires from politics

1989 Publishes her autobiography, *Being Brown*

1993 Becomes chief commissioner of the Ontario Human Rights Commission

1996 Is named an Officer of the Order of Canada

Early Years

Born in Jamaica, Rosemary was the second of three children. Her father died when she was three years old. Rosemary, along with her brother and sister, was raised "in a family of powerful women" by her mother, grandmother, and aunts. Her grandmother helped Rosemary believe that she could accomplish anything.

Rosemary craved attention from others. She often performed and gave speeches to her family on the porch. Rosemary's family encouraged her from a young age to get a good education. Knowledge was more important to them than wealth and fame.

Rosemary spent many summer vacations with her Aunt Lil, who worked in **social welfare** for the Jamaican government. Aunt Lil taught Rosemary that all people, whether they were rich or poor, deserved to be treated with respect.

Rosemary spent her last two years of high school in Kingston, the capital of Jamaica. She went to the same private school that her mother and aunts had attended. The family wanted Rosemary to go to university. They thought she should continue her studies in Canada.

As a child, Rosemary enjoyed music, poetry, and swimming. She loved to spend time playing with her friend, Rex the dog.

Backgrounder

Jamaica

Jamaica is both a nation and an island. It lies in the West Indies. For three hundred years, the country was a colony of Great Britain. This meant that important decisions affecting Jamaica were made in Britain. In 1962, Jamaica became independent. Today, it is an independent nation within the Commonwealth.

Developing Skills

Rosemary arrived in Montreal in 1950. Almost immediately, she experienced racial **prejudice**. Rosemary was given a single room at school because no white students wanted to room with her. At dinner, Rosemary sat at a table with other black students. None of the other girls would talk to her. This was especially difficult for the talkative Rosemary.

Rosemary had never experienced anything like this. She and her family had heard that there was not much racism in Canada. Despite these difficulties, Rosemary did well in school and made friends with other black students. During her second year, she met American student Bill Brown. Bill came to Canada to escape **segregation** policies in the United States. They fell in love and married in 1955.

Rosemary and Bill settled in Vancouver, where Bill studied medicine. They had trouble finding anyone who would rent an apartment to them. They soon joined the British Columbia Association for the Advancement of Coloured Peoples (BCAACP). The BCAACP supported black people in the province by trying to make housing and education more available to them. The organization tried to increase awareness of the problems of racism.

Rosemary met Bill at a meeting of the West Indian Society at McGill University. They were married on August 12, 1955.

Backgrounder

Segregation

Segregation was an important issue in the United States in the 1950s. Segregation meant that African Americans had to go to different schools than whites. They were not allowed to eat in the same restaurants. In 1955, Rosa Parks, an African-American woman, was arrested when she refused to give up her seat on the bus to a white man. The efforts of people, such as human rights **activist** Martin Luther King, Jr., helped change laws in the United States. The Supreme Court finally ruled that segregation in schools was unconstitutional.

When Rosemary and Bill began their family, they wondered if Canada was a good place to raise children. In Jamaica, their children would not experience as much racism. In the end, they decided that Canada was the best place for them to live, and they became Canadian citizens in 1959.

Rosemary got a job with the Children's Aid Society. She loved her job and decided to become a social worker. Rosemary went back to university to earn two more degrees. She set up a volunteer training program for a suicide prevention centre. She also worked as a student counsellor at Simon Fraser University.

Rosemary soon became interested in women's rights. She was one of the founding members of the Vancouver Status of Women Council. She became the **ombudswoman** for the organization, which meant she looked into people's complaints about government bodies.

> We need lots of different experiences and people in our legislatures. Think about (politics) as a marvelous opportunity to do something. In terms of changing the world, it is where it's at. It is the most effective way of bringing change about.

In the late 1960s, Rosemary became aware of the problems facing women in Canada. She soon decided that she could make a difference by entering politics.

Accomplishments

As she became more involved in community issues, Rosemary realized that the best way to make positive change was to run for political office. In 1972, she was elected to the British Columbia legislature. She was the first black woman elected to political office in Canada. In her new position, Rosemary wanted to improve the situation for women, minorities, and the poor.

Rosemary was elected to the British Columbia legislature on August 30, 1972. She represented the riding of Vancouver-Burrard in government.

Rosemary's political party, the New Democratic Party, led the B.C. government. Rosemary had hoped to be given a **Cabinet** position. She also requested a special women's ministry to look into the status of women in B.C. Neither of these dreams came true. Instead, Rosemary had to be content to make changes as a member of the legislature.

Human rights were at the top of Rosemary's list of changes to make. She wanted to make laws that would protect people from being **discriminated** against because of race, religion, gender, economic status, or disability. She soon found out that making any changes took a lot of hard work. Eventually, the government passed legislation that protected human rights.

> ❝ I've been so lucky. I've had so many wonderful opportunities to do things. They far outdistanced my aspirations. I was just part of the movement, the peace movement, the women's movement, the civil rights movement. ❞

▷▷▷▷▷▷

Quick Notes

▷ Rosemary and Bill have three children: Cleta, Gary, and Jonathan.
▷ In 1988, Rosemary was featured in a National Film Board film, *No Way, Not Me.*
▷ Rosemary has sat on the boards of the Canadian Women's Foundation and the South African Educational Trust Fund.

In 1975, Rosemary announced that she would run for leadership of the federal New Democratic Party. For the next several months she travelled across the country campaigning for support. Although she lost to Ed Broadbent, it was a close race. She returned to her position in the B.C. legislature. Rosemary was popular with the constituents in her provincial riding. She was re-elected to the legislature in 1975 and 1979.

In 1996, Rosemary received the Order of Canada for her fourteen years of political service. Governor General Romeo LeBlanc presented the award at a ceremony in Ottawa.

After fourteen years, Rosemary retired from politics in 1986. That year, she became a professor of women's studies at Simon Fraser University. She also continued to fight for human rights in different ways. Rosemary has represented Canada at many conferences on women's issues, including the International Women's Conference on Peace in 1987. In 1989, she began working with MATCH International Centre, a Canadian organization that works to improve the situation of women in Third World nations.

From 1993 to 1996, Rosemary was the chief commissioner of the Ontario Human Rights Commission. She has also served five years on the Canadian Security Intelligence Review Committee, which evaluates the operations and looks at complaints about the Canadian Security Intelligence Service (CSIS). Rosemary continues to speak out about human rights, peace, and women's issues in Canada and around the world.

Backgrounder

Canadian Security Intelligence Service (CSIS)

CSIS is a government agency concerned with protecting Canada's national security. The agency collects and analyzes any information or intelligence on activities that may threaten the security of Canada and warns the government of any potential dangers. Public safety is the main concern of CSIS. Most of its resources are devoted to fighting terrorist actions in Canada.

1924-

June Callwood

> **When I would come across something as a journalist, if something didn't look fair, I'd get people to help change it.**

Key Events

1941 Becomes a reporter for the *Brantford Expositor*

1942 Begins working for the *Globe and Mail*

1957 Publishes her first book called *A Woman Doctor Looks at Life and Love*

1964 Helps found the Civil Liberties Association

1974 Co-founds Nellie's Hostel for Women

1978 Co-chairs the First National Conference on Human Rights

1984 Founds Jessie's Centre for Teenagers

1984 Is inducted into the Canadian News Hall of Fame

1986 Is named Officer of the Order of Canada

1988 Founds the Casey House, a hospice for AIDS patients

1991–96 Hosts *June Callwood's National Treasures* television program

1998 Hosts *Caregiving With June Callwood* television program

Early Years

June Callwood was born in Belle River, Ontario. June's mother was French Canadian and Roman Catholic. Her father was English Canadian and the only Protestant in town. At the time, this was considered a mixed marriage, and June felt different from the other children as a result. This difference she felt helped June to be more accepting of all people later in life. As she said, "I was enough of an outsider myself to help me understand someone who is not accepted."

When June was thirteen years old, her father left the family. This put financial strain on June's mother. It was very difficult for her to support her two daughters alone. At the age of sixteen, June quit high school and moved away from home. She found a job working as a reporter for the *Brantford Expositor* newspaper. Two years later, June worked briefly for a larger newspaper, the *Toronto Star.* June later found a reporting job with the national newspaper, the *Globe and Mail.*

June started her first newspaper job when she was just a teenager.

Backgrounder

Canada's National Newspaper

The *Globe and Mail* newspaper, which calls itself "Canada's National Newspaper," had its beginnings over a century ago. *The Globe* newspaper was first published in 1844, and it had a **circulation** of 300. Seven years later, its circulation was 6,000. *The Globe* soon became known for its excellent articles on national and international news. In 1936, the Globe merged with another newspaper, the *Mail and Empire* to become the *Globe and Mail.* In 1967, the newspaper began to publish Canada's first national daily business paper, the *Report on Business.* In 1979, the *Globe and Mail* became the first newspaper in the world to create a computer database containing all of their articles and to publish electronic and paper versions of the newspaper on the same day. In 1998, the circulation of the *Globe and Mail* was 330,679.

Developing Skills

While working at the *Globe and Mail*, June met a fellow journalist, Trent Frayne. They married in 1944. In her marriage with Trent, June found some of the stability that she felt was missed in her own childhood.

June flew in a U.S. Air Force B-47 while researching a story for *Maclean's* magazine.

After a couple of years, June quit her job at the *Globe and Mail*. She wanted to devote the next several years to raising her four children. When the children were older, June began her career as a freelance journalist.

Soon, June was writing articles and columns for national magazines such as *Maclean's* and *Chatelaine*. Her writing began to focus on social issues of the day. She mostly wrote articles on topics that were not often discussed, such as child abuse.

> 66 *We're living in a time when some choose to watch things go wrong, rather than step in and make change. All big change starts with small individual efforts, done because one human being can't bear to watch bad things happen to another.* 99

During the 1960s, June continued to work as a freelance journalist. She also became a social activist and helped create many organizations to assist people in trouble. In 1964, June helped found the Canadian Civil Liberties Association. A few years later she helped create a home, the Yorkville Digger House, for people living on the street.

June was also concerned about family violence. In 1974, she was a cofounder of Nellie's Hostel for Women. Nellie's is an organization that provides shelter and assistance for women and children who are abused or homeless.

As a journalist, June interviewed many famous people, including singer and actor Harry Belafonte.

Backgrounder

The Canadian Civil Liberties Association

In 1964, a group of Ontario citizens formed the Canadian Civil Liberties Association (CCLA) to protest a proposed law giving police a great deal of power. The CCLA felt the law would not protect people from being harassed by the police. Because of pressure from the CCLA, the bill was withdrawn. The CCLA has since been active in supporting democratic rights by speaking out on issues such as censorship. During the October Crisis of 1970, the CCLA fought against the War Measures Act, which allowed people to be arrested without being formally charged with a crime. Many well-known Canadians have been members of the CCLA, including Pierre Berton, Barbara Frum, and Edward Greenspan.

Accomplishments

June continued to create organizations that helped people who needed it. In 1984, she started up an organization for teenage mothers called Jessie's Centre for Teenagers. The centre is a place where young women can drop in for support and education. In 1988, June founded Casey House, one of the first hospices in Canada for people with AIDS. The home was named after June's youngest son, Casey, who was killed in a motorcycle accident in 1982.

June's hard work and dedication to people has been recognized by many. She was made a Member of the Order of Canada in 1978 and then an Officer of the Order of Canada in 1986. June is recognized for her fight for the underdog. She wants to makes sure that everyone is given a fair chance, regardless of who the person is. A sixteen-year-old broke into June's home and stole her Order of Canada medal and many other items. When the police arrested the thief, June made sure that the teen got a lawyer.

June (left) was named an Officer of the Order of Canada in 1986.

Backgrounder

AIDS Hospices

AIDS hospices are homes for people dying from AIDS. The people who live in the hospices have nowhere else to go and are cared for by volunteers and medical staff. The hospices help AIDS sufferers live out their lives in a homelike environment and die with dignity.

> 66 *I don't have a handle on great truths. I assumed that when I reached a great age, I would know a lot. Well, I've reached 70— somewhere in between calcium supplements and death ... and the fact is, the world seems to be increasingly unknowable.* 99

June has received sixteen honorary degrees and three honorary diplomas. She has given lectures at schools across the country.

In 1998, June hosted a series of programs called *Caregiving with June Callwood.* The series looked at the role of adults in caring for their aging parents. June sees caregiving as a growing social issue in Canada as the population ages. "Right across the country, hospitals are closing beds and trying to get patients out the door in a hurry. But when they go home very often there's nobody there to help."

Helping children has always been one of June's primary interests. She is vice-president of the Campaign Against Child Poverty, an organization that works to reduce the number of poor children in Canada. "I think the rights of the child should start with the right not to be born into poverty and the right not to be abused," she has said.

June holds many honorary university degrees and has written more than twenty-five books during her long career. *Trial Without End: A Shocking Story of Women and AIDS* is about the lives of several women who were all infected with the AIDS virus by the same man.

▶▶▶▶▶▶
QUICK NOTES

▶ June had once planned on becoming a nun.

▶ After her first child was born, June learned how to fly an airplane.

▶ In 1987, June won the humanitarian award from the Ontario Psychological Association.

▶ June was a founding member of the Justice for Children organization.

John Humphrey

1905–1995

> **❝** There is a fundamental connection between human rights and peace. We will have Peace on Earth when everyone's rights are respected. **❞**

Key Events

1929 Receives his fourth university degree

1936 Begins teaching in the Law Faculty at McGill University

1946 Creates the Human Rights Division at the United Nations (UN)

1948 The UN adopts the Universal Declaration of Human Rights

1966 Retires from the UN and returns to McGill

1974 Is named Officer of the Order of Canada

Early Years

Born in Hampton, New Brunswick, John's life there was difficult. When he was only a year old, his father died. At six years old, John had to have his left arm amputated after severely burning it in an accident. Then, John's mother died when he was eleven years old.

John did not let his personal tragedies prevent him from achieving many accomplishments early in his life. He was sent to boarding school, and although he hated it, he was an excellent student. He studied in secret to take the provincial **matriculation** exams early. He was accepted to Mount Allison University at the age of fifteen.

After completing his first degree, John attended McGill University in Montreal. He received three degrees in six years: a Bachelor of Commerce in 1925, a Bachelor of Arts in 1927, and a Bachelor of Civil Law in 1929. After completing his studies, he worked as a lawyer for several years. In 1936, John became a professor in the Faculty of Law at McGill.

John spent much of his life at McGill University—first as a student and later as a professor. McGill is one of Canada's most prestigious universities.

Backgrounder

McGill University

McGill is a university in downtown Montreal, Quebec. It first began with a Faculty of Medicine in 1829. McGill added a Faculty of Arts in 1843, and several other programs were added over the years. The university began admitting female students in 1884. Many famous Canadians graduated from McGill, including astronaut Julie Payette. In 1999, another former graduate, Dr. Marie-Eve Raguenaud, was chosen by Médecins Sans Frontières (Doctors Without Borders) to receive the Nobel Prize for Peace on its behalf.

Developing Skills

John was interested in social justice and equality. While teaching at McGill University, John met Henri Laugier, a professor who taught at the Université de Montréal. The United Nations (UN) was formed after World War II, and Henri later became the Assistant Secretary-General, responsible for Social Affairs. In 1946, Henri asked John to set up the Human Rights Division of the United Nations. John accepted and became the first director of the division.

With the United Nations, John (right) met with many important diplomats, including UN Secretary-General Dag Hammarskjold (centre) and Under-Secretary Phillipe de Seynes (left).

One of John's first tasks was to work with the United Nations Commission on Human Rights to create an International Bill of Rights. This document was to declare the basic rights of every human being. Eleanor Roosevelt, the chairperson of the human rights division, asked John to write the first **draft** of the Declaration of Human Rights.

John spent many weeks producing a 400-page document. His draft contained a bill of rights, suggestions by **delegates** from many nations and organizations, and forty-eight items. The draft was a result of hundreds of suggestions from government delegations, organizations, and individuals. It also included aspects from the laws of many countries that were members of the United Nations.

Backgrounder

The United Nations

In 1945, delegates from around the world met in San Francisco. They wanted to create an organization to preserve peace and protect human rights through international cooperation and collective security. Member countries of the United Nations must agree to accept the UN Charter. The Charter is an international **treaty** that includes the principles of international cooperation. Almost every country in the world, 188 in total, are members of the UN.

In 1948, John discussed the issue of women's rights during a meeting of the UN Economic and Social Council.

John covered all aspects of human rights in his declaration, including civil and political rights, as well as social, cultural, and economic rights. John's draft declaration went to various committees for changes and approvals. The final declaration contained thirty articles protecting the rights of people everywhere.

The General Assembly of the United Nations officially adopted the Declaration of Human Rights on December 10, 1948. Since then, many countries have used the document as the basis for their human rights laws. The International Court uses the document when they pass their judgments. The declaration is also considered to be an expression of the United Nations' global commitment to freedom. Pope John Paul II has referred to the document as "the cornerstone and **conscience** of [humankind]."

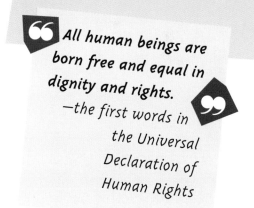

All human beings are born free and equal in dignity and rights.
—the first words in the Universal Declaration of Human Rights

Accomplishments

▶▶▶▶▶▶▶

QUICK NOTES

▶ John earned four university degrees.

▶ Well-known writer Stephen Leacock, who was one of John's economics professors, helped John get into the law program at McGill.

▶ John taught classes until the year before his death at the age of 89.

Despite the fact that he had clearly written the blueprint for the UN declaration, John downplayed his role. He was always modest about his role in writing the basis for the Universal Declaration of Human Rights. Other diplomats were credited with creating the document. John simply claimed that he was among hundreds of people who contributed to the Declaration of Human Rights.

John worked at the United Nations for twenty years. During that time, he continued working to improve human rights worldwide. He was well respected by others because of his great knowledge of international law and his fairness. Some of John's ideas proved to be ahead of their time. In 1963, he suggested that there be a UN high commissioner for human rights. The commissioner would be the human rights representative on the UN **secretariat**. This idea did not come into effect for another thirty years.

John spoke about human rights during a visit to Buenos Aires, Argentina, in 1958.

> **❝** A remarkable person, my husband was an international public servant, a lawyer, a teacher, a writer, but most importantly—a humanitarian. His lifelong commitment to human rights never faltered. **❞**
>
> —Dr. Margaret Kunstler Humphrey after her husband's death

In 1966, John retired from the United Nations. He returned to teaching in the law faculty at McGill. He taught into his eighties. John continued to promote human rights in Canada and around the world. He worked on many international commissions looking into human rights violations. On one fact-finding mission, he travelled to the Philippines to investigate human rights issues that occurred while President Marcos was in power.

On December 10, 1973, the UN held a special meeting to mark the twenty-fifth anniversary of the Declaration of Human Rights. John made a speech to the General Assembly on this special occasion.

Along with other colleagues, John helped create the Canadian Human Rights Foundation. The Foundation is a non-profit organization that works to educate people in Canada and around the world about human rights. John also helped create the Canadian chapter of Amnesty International. This international organization works to prevent human rights violations by governments.

John's work on the Declaration of Human Rights has become well known in recent years. He has received many honours. At McGill, the John P. Humphrey Best Delegation Award is given to the best group that participates in the model United Nations. In 1974, John was named an Officer of the Order of Canada, "in recognition of his contributions to legal scholarship and his world-wide reputation in the field of human rights."

Backgrounder

The John Humphrey Freedom Award

Each year, the International Centre for Human Rights and Democratic Development awards the John Humphrey Freedom Award to an organization or person for "exceptional achievement in the defence or promotion of human rights and democratic development." The award is presented on International Human Rights Day, December 10th. The award includes a prize of $25,000.

1983–

Craig Kielburger

> **"** I think the world could do with more idealists and dreamers. It was the dreamers who thought the Berlin Wall would fall; that women should have the right to vote; that apartheid in South Africa would end. **"**

Key Events

1995 Starts the Free the Children organization to help fight child slavery worldwide

1995–96 Spends eight weeks in South Asia to learn more about the child workers in that region

1996 Meets with Prime Minister Jean Chrétien in Asia to discuss Canada's role in eliminating child slavery

1996 Appears on *60 Minutes*

1998 Is awarded the Roosevelt Institute's Freedom Medal

Early Years

Craig Kielburger was the younger of Fred and Theresa Kielburger's two boys. His early childhood in Thornhill, Ontario, was happy. His parents taught their sons a strong work ethic and an understanding that life can have difficult challenges. Craig's life was much like that of other young people his age. He enjoyed scouting, school, playing video games, hanging out with friends, and playing basketball and floor hockey.

Craig's older brother, Marc, was Craig's role model. When Marc was thirteen, he became interested in protecting the environment. He started **petitions**, gave speeches, and won awards for his environmental work.

Craig (third from left) loved camping and canoeing with his scout troop.

Marc's activism affected Craig. By watching his brother's involvement in issues, Craig realized children have power. When he was only seven years old, Craig helped his older brother gather names for petitions. Because of a speech problem, he had trouble speaking to people. Despite this, Craig enjoyed talking with people. "Someday," he would tell his mother, "I will give speeches." With help from a speech therapist and a lot of work, he learned how to speak properly by the age of ten.

Backgrounder

Petitions

Petitions are documents that are used to encourage governments or other organizations or businesses to change policies or laws. People sign their names and addresses to petitions if they agree with what the petition is about. Petitions are usually required to have a certain number of signatures on them to be valid.

Developing Skills

At eleven, Craig entered his first public speaking competition. His speech was called "What It Means to Be a Winner." He was so nervous he forgot his speech. Instead, he made up a new one. He spoke from his heart, talking about the importance of fighting for what you believe in, even when there are obstacles. As Craig spoke, he became more confident. The audience applauded loudly after he was done. Craig won the gold medal. He entered and won several other public speaking contests.

When he was in the seventh grade, Craig attended a meeting to discuss the closure of the local library. After many adults spoke on the issue, Craig stood up and talked about how important the library was to children in the community. Craig made some very convincing arguments. He was asked to speak at another meeting to help save the library. The library is still open and is run with help from volunteers. Craig learned that young people could be heard. All that was needed, he learned, was knowledge about an issue and the confidence to speak up.

At age twelve, Craig inspired other kids at his school to become involved in human rights issues.

Backgrounder

Iqbal Masih

When Iqbal Masih was four years old, his parents sold him to a carpet manufacturer because they could not afford to support him. For six years, Iqbal was forced to work long hours every day. He was often chained to his loom. He squatted all day and was not fed well. Because of this, he did not grow properly. Iqbal was freed from his slavery when he was ten.

April 19, 1995 started as a normal day for Craig. As he ate breakfast before school, he turned to the newspaper to read the comics. The front page had an article about a twelve-year-old boy who had been murdered. The boy, Iqbal Masih, had escaped a life of child slavery in Pakistan. He had travelled around the world to inform people of the mistreatment of children in his country.

Craig (middle back) and other members of Free the Children collected many signatures for their petition to stop child labour in developing countries.

Craig was shocked that something so terrible could happen to a boy his age. He did not even know that child slavery existed. After school, he went to the public library to learn more about child labour. What he learned upset him deeply. In some parts of the world, children as young as four were made to do difficult work for many hours a day. Many children were hurt or killed doing dangerous work in factories.

Craig also learned that little was being done to stop child labour around the world. He contacted several human rights organizations. He found out that a group called Youth Action Network was sponsoring an event that weekend. The next day in school, he asked his teacher if he could speak to the class for a few minutes. He stood up and told the class what he had learned about child labour. He also asked if any other students wanted to join him to start a group to help eliminate child labour. That night, several students met at Craig's house to plan a display for the weekend event. The Free the Children (FTC) organization was born.

> Everyone has the power to change the world by helping one person at a time, whether you're eight or eighty years old.

Accomplishments

Craig and FTC were a success at the Youth Action Network's event. The group started to go to city schools to let other children know what was happening around the world. Young people representing the FTC began to speak to students in much higher grades. At first, the older students asked questions about child labour that Craig and the others found hard to answer. Craig did not let this stop him. He and the group researched the topics and sent letters to the classes answering their questions.

Craig and FTC were beginning to attract the attention of larger groups of people. A television producer made a documentary on the group. In fall of 1995, Craig spoke to a group of two thousand people at a labour convention. That night, the delegates pledged $150,000 to help FTC build a centre to feed child labourers. The next day, the *Toronto Star* had a photo of Craig and FTC with their petition on the front page.

A few months later, Craig was given the opportunity to travel to five countries in South Asia. At first, his parents were concerned that the trip would not be safe for their son. Eventually, Craig convinced his parents of the importance of the trip.

Craig has travelled to more than thirty countries around the world. On his journeys, he talks to children to learn more about their living conditions.

Craig travelled the countries with a chaperone. The eight weeks in Asia opened Craig's eyes to how bad the child labour situation was in South Asia. Craig tried to speak with as many children as possible to assess their situations. He met many young children who worked as many as twelve hours a day without any breaks or holidays. Many of the children told stories about how they were abused if they fell asleep at their workplace. Some worked in very dangerous environments.

Upon returning to Canada, Craig was even more convinced of the importance of the work done by the Free the Children organization. He encouraged other Canadians to be aware that some of the things we own, such as name brand clothing and carpet, were made by child slaves in developing countries. FTC pressured Canada to adopt the Rugmark system.

In 1998, Craig and eight other FTC members travelled to India for twelve days. During this trip, Craig saw some of the children he met on his first trip. Because of his work, many of these children led better lives than they had before.

> Children aren't simply empty vessels waiting to be filled; we're people with ideas, talents, opinions, and dreams.

Craig shares his interest in human rights with many people, including the Dalai Lama of Tibet.

Backgrounder

Rugmark

The Rugmark system began in Asia. Many child labourers in this region are forced to work long hours to make carpets by hand. Any carpets made using fair labour practices are marked with a Rugmark label. Consumers who purchase carpets with this label can then be sure that they are not supporting child labour.

Emily Murphy

> The world loves a peaceful [person], but gives way to a strenuous kicker.

Key Events

1887   Marries Arthur Murphy

1889   Family moves to England where Emily writes her first *Janey Canuck* book

1901   Moves to Swan River, Manitoba, where Emily writes for magazines

1907   Moves to Edmonton

1910   Is first woman appointed to the Edmonton Hospital Board

1916   Is appointed first woman police magistrate in British Empire

1922   Writes *The Black Candle* concerning the drug trade in Canada

1927   Begins her fight to have women considered persons under Canadian law

Early Years

Emily Ferguson grew up in Cookstown, Ontario, with her parents and four siblings. Emily and her two older brothers spent their days exploring the woods around their home. They often got into trouble for such things as stealing apples from their neighbour's yards. Emily's father encouraged her to do the same things as her brothers did. She was expected to do the same chores, such as piling up wood and weeding the garden. Emily's mother was unhappy to have such a tomboy for a daughter.

At the age of seven, Emily began to go to a one-room school. Because he wanted the best for his children, her father hired tutors to teach them Latin, penmanship, and music. Education was very important in their home. Political issues were often discussed around the family's dinner table. Prime Minister John A. Macdonald was a family friend and would sometimes visit the Fergusons.

At fourteen, Emily moved to Toronto to attend boarding school. She worked hard at school and her favorite subjects were literature, botany, and sports. While at school, Emily met Arthur Murphy, who was studying to become a minister. The two fell in love. With her parent's approval, Emily married Arthur in 1887.

Emily came from Cookstown, Ontario, a small town north of Toronto.

Backgrounder

John A. Macdonald

Born in Scotland, John A. Macdonald moved to Upper Canada with his parents when he was five years old. He graduated from school at the age of fourteen and then worked as a lawyer. Macdonald was one of the "Fathers of Confederation" who helped create the British North America Act. This in turn created the country of Canada. He became the nation's first prime minister in 1867. One of his main goals was to create a nation that spread across the entire continent.

Developing Skills

As a minister's wife, Emily was expected to set an example. She taught Bible classes, spoke at religious meetings and arranged fundraising events. She found the time to read and help Arthur with his sermons. Emily was more opinionated and outspoken than most women of the time. However, she was also kind and had a good sense of humor. The Murphys and their three daughters moved several times over the next decade.

Emily's life changed when Arthur decided to become a missionary. They sold most of their belongings, packed up the rest, and travelled from town to town so Arthur could preach. Emily missed her old life but made the best of her new one. She wrote about many of the humorous things she saw. Arthur was very successful. The family was sent to England where he could work as a missionary.

Emily was excited to see England, but she was saddened by the poverty. England was in the middle of the Industrial Revolution. Emily saw disease, garbage in the streets, and beggars. She saw the differences between the lives of the very poor and the very rich. She tried to learn as much about the lives of the poor as possible. Emily decided to write a book, *Impressions of Janey Canuck Abroad*, to inform people about the injustices she witnessed in England.

Emily (right) enjoyed spending time with her daughters, Evelyn and Kathleen.

Backgrounder

The Industrial Revolution

The Industrial Revolution was the era when Western society moved from being an agricultural society to a modern, industrial society. In England, the Industrial Revolution took place from about 1750 to 1850. Social and economic changes took place in England as new technologies such as the steam engine helped create factories that could produce goods on a large scale. The population, which had mostly been farmers, increasingly moved into cities and towns to work in the factories.

After three years, the Murphy family returned to Canada. Emily's *Janey Canuck* book was published, and it became popular in both England and Canada. She also began to write for several small magazines. Emily was forced to work more when Arthur became very sick. She wrote day and night to make enough money to support the family. Then tragedy struck. Their youngest daughter died of **diphtheria**. Emily and Arthur decided to move west and start a new life.

In Manitoba, Emily quickly became active in social issues. She pressured the government to build a hospital in the town. She interviewed many Western people and wrote three books about cultures of Western Canada.

Emily's experiences made her realize that although it was not recognized by the government, women were equal to men. She knew women could be useful and contribute to society. At this time, women were not allowed to vote, and they rarely worked outside of the home.

> " We are coming to see that a mother who lets herself subside into a kind of burnt-sacrifice upon what is called the 'family altar' is not really a good mother, nor a good citizen. "

Emily was sworn in as police magistrate for the city of Edmonton in June, 1916.

Accomplishments

Emily's political life began when the family moved to Edmonton. In Alberta, women could not own property. Any money earned by a woman legally belonged to her husband, as did any children. If a man died without a will, the wife was left with nothing. Emily wanted to change these laws. She asked the legislature for more legal protection for women. Although Emily's argument was convincing, the members did not want to support a woman. Emily's ideas were thrown out, but newspapers began to write about her cause. The next year, Emily was successful. The Dower Act of Alberta was passed. It gave wives more rights.

After her success, Emily wanted other reforms. She spoke out on many **controversial** topics and helped pass laws to protect the rights of women, children, prison inmates, young offenders, and the mentally ill. She became well known as a journalist and women's rights supporter.

Emily worked with the Equal Franchise League to help get women the right to vote. In 1916, women in Alberta gained the right to vote in provincial and municipal elections.

That same year, Emily successfully argued that there should be a special court for women. Soon after, Emily became the first female judge in the British Empire. She strove to be fair and **impartial** in her new position.

Emily's busy schedule still left her time to tend to her garden.

▶▶▶▶▶▶

QUICK NOTES

▶ Throughout her life, Emily was active in more than twenty women's organizations, including the National Council of Women and the Canadian Women's Press Club.

▶ Before Emily's *Janey Canuck* books, the word "canuck" was used as an insult. Her books made Canadians proud of the name.

▶ Emily enjoyed painting in her spare time.

Emily loved her work as a judge, but male lawyers often questioned her authority. Female judges and politicians at this time faced many problems. Canada's constitution, the British North America Act, protected the rights of "persons." Many people argued that females were not legally persons. This meant that they could not be judges or politicians

In 1927, Emily decided to get women declared as "persons" once and for all. According to the law, any five Canadian citizens could ask Parliament to answer questions about the constitution. Emily gathered together four other female reformers and went to face the Supreme Court of Canada. These "Famous Five" found a lawyer who was willing to argue in court that women were indeed persons. After five weeks, the Supreme Court declared that women were not legally persons. Women across Canada were shocked by the decision.

The Famous Five would not be stopped and decided to appeal their case to the highest court in the British Empire. The Privy Council in England debated the issue for several months. Because of Emily Murphy and her Famous Five, women across Canada were finally considered "persons" under the law in 1929.

> ❝ She was a humanist. In fact, many of her writings were not purely putting things right for women, but men too. ❞
> —biographer Christine Mander

As a judge, Emily believed that courts should show mercy and work to rehabilitate people who broke the law.

Backgrounder

The British North America (BNA) Act

The BNA Act (sometimes called the Constitution Act) was the legislation that created Canada as a nation separate from Britain in 1867. The act used the pronoun "he" and the term "persons" throughout, with persons referring only to males. The current Canadian Constitution contains the Charter of Rights and Freedoms, which protects the rights of all Canadians, male or female.

MORE GREAT CANADIANS

Here are some more Canadian humanitarians. These people have fought for the rights of others. There are many other Canadian humanitarians. The Suggested Reading List will help you find more information.

1912–1972

Max Bell

Max Bell was a successful businessman and philanthropist. During his life, Max donated money to many community causes. He anonymously gave out many university scholarships to young people and gave money to help support hospitals. Shortly before his death in 1972, Max created the Max Bell Foundation. Since then, the foundation has given out more than $50 million to worthy causes, such as health care and education. The foundation "has always sought to support creative and innovative endeavours that encourage the development of human potential in pursuit of social, academic, and economic goals."

Max Bell

1933–

Thomas Berger

Thomas Berger is a lawyer and former judge of the Supreme Court of Canada. Throughout his career, he has fought for Aboriginal rights in Canada and international human rights issues. In 1971, he successfully argued for the existence of Aboriginal rights for Canadian Aboriginal Peoples. Thomas was made an Officer of the Order of Canada in 1989.

1929–

Gladys Cook

Gladys is a social worker who counsels women and children experiencing abuse or other problems in the Aboriginal community. She is involved with the National Native Alcohol and Drug Abuse program, which helps Aboriginal people whose lives are affected by substance abuse. Gladys also runs suicide prevention workshops. She was awarded the Canada 125 Medal for her commitment to her community and country.

1923–

Jules Deschênes

A chief justice of the Quebec Supreme Court, Jules was also an expert in international law. He served on the United Nation's Sub-Committee on the Prevention of Discrimination and Protection of Minorities. In 1985, he was chairman of the federal inquiry on Nazi war criminals living in Canada. In 1993, he was named a Companion of the Order of Canada. Until he retired in 1997, Jules was a judge on the International Tribunal on War Crimes in former Yugoslavia and Rwanda.

Terry Fox

1958–1981

Terry Fox

In 1977, at the age of eighteen, Terry lost his right leg to cancer. He came up with an idea to run across Canada to raise funds and awareness about the disease. He began the Marathon of Hope in St. John's on April 12, 1980. He ran 5,373 kilometres during his 143-day trek, getting as far as Thunder Bay, Ontario.

Terry had to stop because cancer had returned to his lungs. He died several months later. Every September, many Canadians across the country participate in the Terry Fox Run. This event has raised about $250 million for cancer research.

1958–

Rick Hansen

A world class wheelchair athlete, Rick wheeled around the world from 1985 to 1987. His friend Terry Fox inspired him to start his Man in Motion tour. He wanted to raise money for spinal cord research and rehabilitation. Over the next two years, Rick wore out 117 tires and eleven pairs of gloves. He raised around $20 million as well as awareness about spinal injury.

Since his tour, Rick has been active in promoting post-secondary education for students with physical disabilities. In 1997, he established the Rick Hansen Institute at the University of British Columbia. His aim is to help people with disabilities reach their full potential. Rick was named Companion of the Order of Canada in 1987.

Stephen Lewis

universities and hospitals. Scholarships and fellowships continue to be given to Canadians each year in Izaak Killam's name.

1937–

Stephen Lewis

Stephen Lewis is a former leader of the Ontario New Democratic Party. He wrote an important government report on race relations in Ontario. Stephen went on to write a newspaper column and host television and radio broadcasts.

Stephen acted as Canada's ambassador to the United Nations from 1984 to 1988. He was also named a special advisor to the United Nation's general secretary about African issues in 1986. Stephen had taught English in Africa in the 1950s and was familiar with many of the problems in this region. Since 1995, he has been involved with the United Nations Children Fund (UNICEF), where he is active in urging nations around the world to help end child poverty.

1914–1993

Wilson Head

Wilson was a civil rights activist who dedicated his life to battling racism and supporting human rights. He was born in the United States, where he received a graduate degree in social work. After moving to Canada, he founded the Urban Alliance on Race Relations, an organization that has brought about many improvements. He sat on the board of directors of the Canadian Civil Liberties Association for sixteen years and was active in black organizations and peace groups.

1885–1955

Izaak Killam

Izaak Killam did not learn business at university. He just had the drive to succeed. He made millions of dollars through his businesses. He was said to be the richest Canadian of his day. Izaak was not caught up in his money. After his death, his wife Dorothy carried out his wishes to use his money to assist theatre, education, and the sciences. Fifty million dollars from his estate was used to fund the Canada Council. She donated millions of dollars to

1900-1991

Robert McClure

Robert McClure spent more than fifty years as a medical missionary in Asia and Africa. He often worked in countries during wartime, giving medical assistance to injured civilians and soldiers, feeding and housing refugees, and establishing orphanages. Robert even parachuted out of planes to reach injured soldiers before they were carried to field hospitals. Throughout his life, Bob travelled the world, volunteering his time and expertise to help people who otherwise would not receive medical attention. Bob won the Man of the Year Peace Award.

1911-1995

Mary Two-Axe Earley

Mary was a member of the Mohawk nation. She dedicated her life to changing the federal law that took away Indian Status from any Aboriginal woman who married a non-Aboriginal. She succeeded in 1985. Mary also founded the Equal Rights for Indian Women organization. In 1979, Mary received the Persons Award for her work in improving the quality of life of Canadian women.

1888-1967

Georges Vanier

Considered by *Maclean's* magazine to be the "Most Important Canadian in History," Georges Vanier devoted his life to Canada both in the military and as a Canadian ambassador in France. After fighting in World War I, Major-General Georges Vanier represented Canada at many international conferences, including the League of Nations, an organization set up to prevent future wars.

Georges served as governor general from 1959 to 1967. He was famous for treating everyone equally and for trying to help the disadvantaged. He and his wife travelled across the country to visit with and help Canadians. Georges also worked to improve relations between Quebec and the rest of Canada.

Georges Vanier

GLOSSARY

activist: a person who takes action in support of a particular issue

Cabinet: the advisory board for the government's leader

campaigning: working towards being elected

circulation: the number of copies sold or distributed of a publication

civil rights: basic rights of individuals

conscience: the sense of what is right and wrong

controversial: something that is not of the popular opinion; something that causes argument

delegates: people who represent others

diphtheria: a disease affecting the throat

discriminated: judged on the basis of race, religion, or lifestyle

doctorate: one of the highest academic degrees awarded by universities

draft: the first outline or plan of a document

fellowship: a financial grant made to a visiting graduate student at a university

impartial: fair and unbiased

legislature: a group of people with the duty to make laws for a government

matriculation: enrolling in courses for university or college

ombudswoman: a woman who looks into and helps settle complaints between individual people and organizations or companies

petitions: written documents signed by supporters making a request from a person or organization in power

philanthropists: people who work to improve the condition of other people through donations of money or other types of aid

prejudice: judgment based on stereotypes or inadequate information

secretariat: officials who perform administrative, record-keeping, and secretarial duties of an international organization

segregation: separating people from different ethnic backgrounds in schools, housing, and at the workplace; usually refers to discrimination against visible minorities.

social welfare: government economic assistance to people in need

treaty: a formal agreement between countries. A treaty usually concerns peace or economic trade.

unanimous: when everyone agrees on a particular issue

SUGGESTED READING

Callwood, June. *June Callwood's National Treasures.* Toronto: Stoddart, 1994.

Kielburger, Craig; Kevin Major (Contributor). *Free the Children: A Young Man's Personal Crusade Against Child Labour.* McClelland & Stewart Inc., 1998.

James, Donna. *Emily Murphy.* Don Mills, ON: Fitzhenry & Whiteside, 1977.

Roy, Lynette. *Brown Girl in the Ring: Rosemary Brown.* Toronto: Sister Vision, 1992.

INDEX

activist 14, 21, 44, 46
Amnesty International 29

campaign 4, 8, 17, 23, 46
Canadian Civil Liberties
    Association 21, 44
Canadian Human Rights
    Foundation 29
Canadian Security
    Intelligence Service 17
civil rights 4, 16, 27,
    44, 46

doctorate 6, 7, 46

economics 7, 28

Free the Children (FTC)
    30, 33, 34, 35, 47

Globe and Mail 18, 19, 20

hospice 18, 22
human rights 4, 5, 6, 10,
    11, 12, 14, 16, 17, 18, 24,
    26, 27, 28, 29, 32, 33, 35,
    42, 44

Industrial Revolution 38

John Humphrey Freedom
    Award 10, 29

legislation 16, 41

McGill University 14, 24,
    25, 26, 28, 29

Nellie's Hostel 18, 21
New Democratic Party
    (NDP) 6, 8, 9, 12, 16,
    17, 44

ombudswoman 15, 46
Ontario Human Rights
    Commission 12, 17
Order of Canada 6, 11,
    12, 17, 18, 22, 24, 29,
    42, 43

petition 31, 33, 34, 46
philanthropist 5, 42, 46
prejudice 14, 46

racism 14, 15, 44
Rugmark 35

segregation 14, 46
slavery 30, 32, 33
social welfare 13, 46
Supreme Court 14, 41,
    42, 43

UNICEF 44
United Nations 11, 24, 26,
    27, 28, 29, 43, 44
Universal Declaration of
    Human Rights 24, 26,
    27, 28, 29

women's rights 10, 11,
    15, 40

Youth Action Network
    33, 34